Around the World
in a
BATHTUB

Bathing All Over the Globe

XZ
B

Wade Bradford
Illustrated by Micha Archer

Charlesbridge

To Abigail and her family—W. B.

For Max and Grandpa Bob,
my world travelers—M. A.

This book could not have been made without the expertise of Pallav Chatterjee,
Sharad Dhakal, Sinan Goknur, Yuki Muranaka, Takako Iseda, Ntando Nkala-Sarr,
Scott Wells, and the Yup'ik Museum of Bethel, Alaska—W. B.

Text copyright © 2017 by Wade Bradford
Illustrations copyright © 2017 by Micha Archer
All rights reserved, including the right of reproduction in whole or
in part in any form. Charlesbridge and colophon are registered
trademarks of Charlesbridge Publishing, Inc.

Published by Charlesbridge
85 Main Street
Watertown, MA 02472
(617) 926-0329
www.charlesbridge.com

Illustrations done in oils and custom-made collage papers on gessoed
   paper then manipulated in Photoshop
Display type set in Family Cat Fat by Jakob Fischer at
   www.pizzadude.dk
Text type set in Grenadine MVB © 2003 by Markanna Studios Inc.
Scanning by 5000K Digital Imaging in Pembroke, Massachusetts, USA
Color separations by Colourscan Print Co Pte Ltd, Singapore
Printed by 1010 Printing International Limited in Huizhou,
   Guangdong, China
Production supervision by Brian G. Walker
Designed by Martha MacLeod Sikkema

Library of Congress Cataloging-in-Publication Data
Names: Bradford, Wade, author. | Archer, Micha, illustrator.
Title: Around the world in a bathtub / Wade Bradford;
   illustrated by Micha Archer.
Description: Watertown, MA: Charlesbridge, 2017.
Identifiers: LCCN 2016009215| ISBN 9781580895446
   (reinforced for library use) | ISBN 9781607349471 (ebook) |
   ISBN 9781607349488 (ebook pdf)
Subjects: LCSH: Bathing customs—Juvenile literature.
Classification: LCC GT2845 .B73 2017 | DDC 391.6/4—dc23
   LC record available at https://lccn.loc.gov/2016009215

Printed in China
(hc) 10 9 8 7 6 5 4 3 2 1

Somewhere right now,
water is filling up a bathtub,
steam is fogging up a mirror,
washcloths and rubber duckies are waiting . . .

. . . but a little boy is running through the house.

"Bath time," says the mama.

"No, no!" says the boy.

"Yes, yes," says the mama.

Yes, yes!

A chase begins . . .

This happens all over the world,
but sometimes in different ways.

In Japan, grandmother scrubs granddaughter's cheeks and washes and rinses her hair before she gets into the bathtub. The family members, from oldest to youngest, take turns relaxing in a square tub called an *ofuro*.

In Turkey, families visit an enormous bathhouse called a *hammam*. Attendants scrub the bathers with rough cloths and strong soap. After the scrubbing, the children are given slippers and towels.

They relax inside a sauna. Big sister wears a mask of mud. Now it's time for the twins to put the wet clay all over their faces.

Evet, evet!
(eh-vet)

Hayır, hayır!
(hye-YER)

Hayır, hayır!
(hye-YER)

In India,
many Hindus honor their ancestors
by bathing in the Ganges River.

Father leads son down the steps and into the cool water,
which is a little too cold for this boy's toes.

Haan, haan!
(hahn)

Nahi, nahi!
(NAH-ee)

On the plains of the Alaskan tundra, a Yup'ik family
trudges through the icy wind. They enter a *maqii*, a
small wooden cabin with one door and no windows.
Grandfather stokes a fire to heat the stones.

Qang-a, qang-a!
(kang-nah)

I-ii, i-ii!
(ee)

Little brother watches the steam stretch across the room. Sweat drips and washes him clean. But it is so hot, he would rather be outside in the snow.

For thousands of years, children have said no to bath time, whether running away from a waterfall shower,

or avoiding the oils and perfumes of an Egyptian bath,

And someday in the future, kids will be saying no
to bath time as they float around in a space station.

There are so many places to take a bath, whether in the bogey holes on the Australian coast . . .

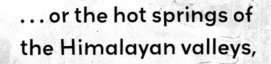

. . . or the hot springs of
the Himalayan valleys,

Ho, ho!
(hoh)

Hoina,
hoina!
(HOY-nah)

whether in the sunny lakes of South Africa . . .

Millions of children around the world take baths every day.

Many of them don't want to at first.

But once they get in . . .

. . . they don't want to get out.

"Can we stay in just a little longer?"
ask the children.

"No, no," say the grown-ups.

"Yes, yes!" say the children.

Yes, yes!

The bath-time battle continues, and it usually ends . . .

...with a **splash!**

Bathing Around the Globe

Japan: Before soaking in an *ofuro*, bathers scrub themselves clean. They rinse themselves thoroughly and then get into the warm, soothing water. Because the family members take turns relaxing in the *ofuro*, it is impolite to get the water soapy or dirty.

Turkey: Bathhouses (*hammams*) in Turkey are cherished for their beautiful stonework and domed ceilings. Guests begin their experience in a room with warm, flowing air. In the next room, the air becomes very hot, and the guests bathe in cold water. Many *hammams* offer soapy scrub treatments and mud masks to help clean and moisturize the bathers' skin.

India: In addition to using modern showers and bathtubs, some Indian families partake in ritual bathing as a religious practice. For many Hindus, the Ganges River and its tributaries are sacred. By taking a "holy dip" in the river, family members honor long-ago ancestors, as well as parents and grandparents who have passed away.

United States (Alaska): Before steam baths became common, male members of ancient Yup'ik tribes would gather in a *qasgiq*, a partially underground structure used as a meeting place for storytelling, ceremonial dances, and sweat baths. A roaring fire heated the room, while smoke billowed up through a hole in the ceiling. A modern-day *maqii* can reach temperatures above 250 degrees Fahrenheit!

Australia: The southeastern coast of Australia features many bogey holes, or "ocean baths," that are popular swimming spots. In the past, these large tide pools were used by Aboriginal people to trap fish. The famous Bogey Hole began as a rocky platform carved by the surf. In the early 1800s workers removed tons of rock to create a private bath. A barricade separates the Bogey Hole from the ocean, which (hopefully) keeps out the sharks!

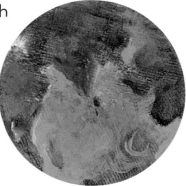

Nepal: Hot springs are scattered among the Himalayan valleys. These natural bathing spots are formed when water deep within the earth's crust heats up and rises to the surface. Some Nepalese hot springs have been surrounded with stone walls, becoming the main attraction of the village. Others are found at the end of difficult trails, but adventurous hikers say they're worth the trek.

South Africa: Johannesburg and other South African cities are home to modern bathtubs, swimming pools, and aquatic centers. In more rural areas, beyond the reach of indoor plumbing, many children bathe in rivers, streams, ponds, and lakes. In desert regions, clean water is scarce, so boreholes are dug to create wells for drinking and bathing water.

Colombia: Normally, if someone asks you to jump into a volcano, you should say no. However, in northern Colombia there is an unusual place called Volcán de Lodo El Totumo. It's a short mud volcano (only fifty feet in height) with wooden stairs that climb to the top. Visitors in bathing suits take a dip in the warm mud and then hop into the nearby lagoon to wash off.

The Ancient World: Many ancient empires, including the Roman, Greek, and Egyptian civilizations, constructed bathhouses with beautiful statues, towering pillars, and other amazing architectural features. In a city in England, you can visit magnificent Roman ruins that were built around a hot spring. Can you guess the name of the city? Bath!

International Space Station: Water can be a tricky thing in zero gravity. If astronauts tried to take a shower, the water would float everywhere! Instead, they squeeze a mixture of water and soap out of a small bag. The soapy water forms spheres that stick to skin. The astronauts also use a lot of baby wipes.

A note about language: Every language has its variations. Depending on where you live and who you're talking to, you might say "yes" or "no" differently from the characters in this book. That's part of the fun of language!